THE EYE
Nature's camera

Eyes come in lots of different shapes. Human eyes are round like a ball. Other animals can have flattened or tube-shaped eyes.

·············· Simple eyes ··············   Compound eyes

Human   Eagle   Lizard   Ant

How the human eye works

The lens is a see-through layer of tissue that focuses the light. Many animals can change the shape of the lens to focus on objects at different distances.

The cornea is a thick, see-through covering that protects the eye.

The iris is a ring of muscles that can open or close. This lets more or less light through the hole in its center, called **the pupil**.

The retina is a thin layer at the back of the eye. It is covered in light-sensitive cells called **photoreceptors** that capture light and detect color. Humans have more than 130 million photoreceptors in each eye.

The image is upside down on **the retina** but our brains turn it the right way up.

Photoreceptor cells come in two types:
• **rods**, which allow us to see lightness and darkness;
• **cones**, which allow us to see color.

The fovea centralis is the most light-sensitive part of the retina. More photoreceptors are concentrated here than anywhere else. This allows it to capture the sharpest image.

Seeing with your brain

We don't just see with our eyes—we need our brains to decode the information.

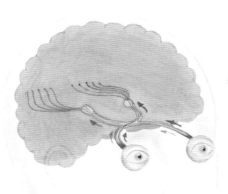

• **First**, the rods and cones break down the image into electrical signals that are sent to the brain.

• **Each side** of the brain receives information from both eyes.

• **The brain interprets** this information and creates an image.

• **The whole journey** from eye to brain takes less than a second.

HOW DO WE SEE?

Below is a scene viewed through human eyes. But what about the other animals in the picture? Do they see the same thing? (If you leave this page folded out to the side you can compare the different scenes.)

Some animals have a wide field of vision, but others have a narrow one. Some see fast movements, and others can only perceive motion when it's slow. Some animals see the world in many colors; others only see one or two. Some can make out lots of detail; others move through a world of fuzzy shapes.

3

Look out for the symbols below to learn more about how animals see.

Field of vision

How much of their surroundings animals see depends on where their eyes are on their heads. Predators, such as tigers and wolves, have eyes that face forward. They see very well in front of them. Prey animals, such as deer and cows, have eyes on the sides of their heads. They see much better what's around them, keeping a lookout for hungry predators.

180 degrees   360 degrees

Humans have a field of vision of 200 degrees. This means we see just over half of the circle around us. This system allowed our ancestors to spot danger to the sides. Our vision has three areas. In the one on each side we see with only one eye. But in the area in the center we see with both eyes at once (called binocular vision). In this zone we see objects in 3-D and judge distances best.

Capturing movement

To see movement, our eyes take still snapshots. Then our brain puts them together to make a sequence. Humans take about twenty of these snapshots per second. But some animals take as few as four snapshots per second. This means they can only see much slower movements than we do. Others take as many as 300. They can see movements so fast that they are invisible or very blurry to us.

Light and color

When light enters our eyes, it hits the surface at the back of the eyeball. This surface, the retina, is covered in special cells that capture light. There are two types of these cells, called rods and cones. Rod cells only detect light's brightness. But cone cells detect wavelengths of light and convert them to colors. We are used to the rainbow of colors we see, but many animals' cone cells are different from ours. This means some see fewer colors than we do. Others see lots more, including ultraviolet and infrared.

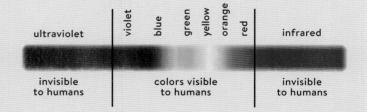

ultraviolet	violet	blue	green	yellow	orange	red	infrared

invisible to humans   colors visible to humans   invisible to humans

Sharp or blurry

Some animals can see in sharp focus. Others travel through a blurry world. For most animals in this book, sharpness depends on three things: the size of the eye, the shape of the lens that focuses light, and the number of rod and cone cells on the back of the eye.

CONTENTS

WHAT ANIMALS SEE
The world through animals' eyes

Do dogs see in color? Can cats really see at night? How do insects find flowers? Which animals have better vision than we do?

Scientists perform experiments to learn how animals see. They have looked through the eyes of bugs, painted beehives different colors, and shown pictures to chimpanzees. They have even released bats into the air with blindfolds on!

Scientists have learned a lot from this research. But there is still plenty to discover. Let's take a look at the world through animals' eyes!

Why see at all?

That depends on the animal!
Sight can help animals explore, find food, escape from predators, and avoid bumping into things. It can aid a predator in catching its prey or a bee in its search for flowers. Sight can also help animals find members of the same species and communicate with them.

Other senses

Animals have lots of senses for finding their way through the world. Vision is important for humans and other apes. But many animals depend on other senses. Smell, taste, hearing, or touch can be just as important. If an animal can't see well, its other senses are often more developed.

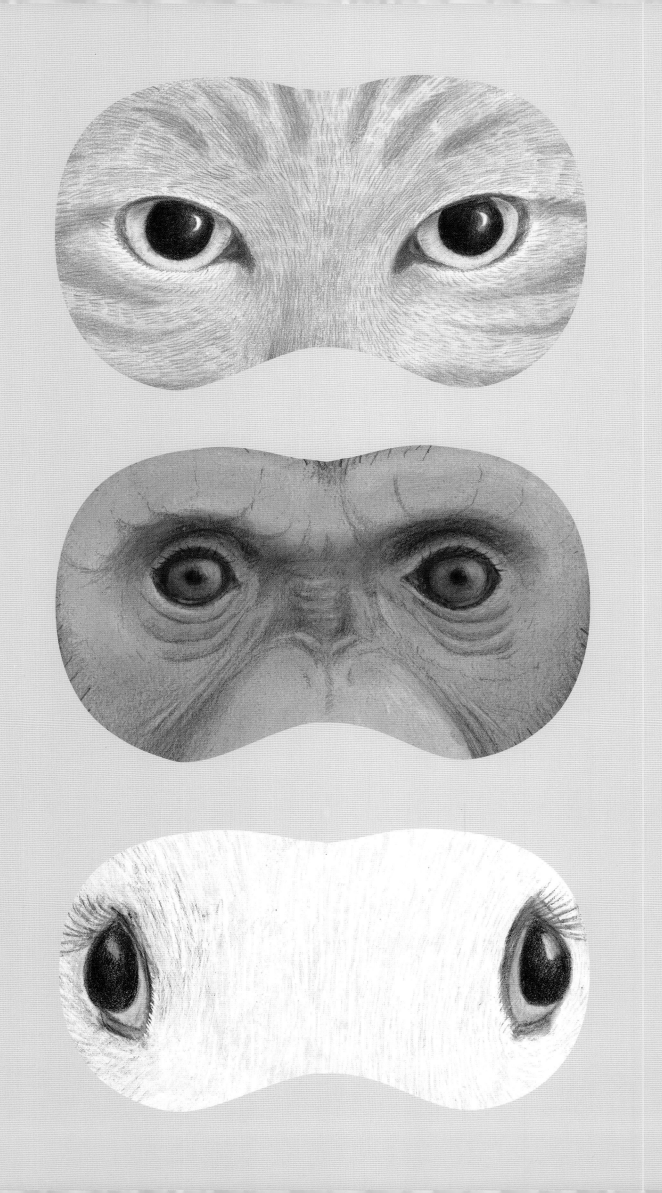

MAMMALS
THREE COLORS OR TWO?

Mammals grow hair or fur and feed their babies milk produced from their bodies. Plus, nearly all mammals give birth to live young instead of laying eggs. We know of about 5,000 species of mammals. This group includes cats, dogs, mice, horses, elephants, platypuses . . . and humans!

Some mammals have great vision, and some see poorly or are even blind. But all mammals have senses which help them to survive. Many meat-eating mammals hunt at the end of the day thanks to good vision in low light. Some prey mammals have eyes on the sides of their heads. This gives them a wide field of vision, so they can spot predators and hide before being gobbled up.

Humans are trichromats, which means they see in three colors. These colors can mix together to make many others. But imagine a world where red is seen as yellow or green. Like some color-blind humans, most mammals are dichromats, which means they can only see a mixture of two colors.

The colors seen by a trichromat, such as a human. The retinas of trichromats have three types of cone cells.

The colors seen by a dichromat, which includes most mammals. Dichromats only have two types of cone cells in their retinas.

CHIMPANZEE
Almost like us

For primates (such as monkeys, lemurs, and humans), vision is important for moving about and finding food. Chimpanzees are some of our closest cousins among animals. So, does this mean they see the world just like we do?

DOG

Color-blind predator

Dogs' keen senses have been passed down from their ancestors, wolves. Their sense of smell is among the best in the animal kingdom. Plus, their incredible hearing allows them to pick up infrasound and ultrasound—sounds that humans can't hear. But when it comes to sight, dogs have a mixed record.

CAT

The eyes of a hunter

Cats see five times less clearly than humans. But this doesn't stop them being fierce predators. Unfortunately for mice and birds, cats are supersensitive to movement and light. So sensitive, in fact, that they can hunt equally well at night as in the day.

RABBIT & SQUIRREL

Always on alert

These small prey mammals use their strong sense of smell to stay alert for predators. Smell also helps them sniff out food hidden in fields or on the forest floor. Rabbits and squirrels don't have vision as clear as ours. But with eyes on the sides of their heads, they can spot predators closing in and escape.

BAT
Sound and vision

Bats rely on a special sense for finding their way around. Most of them can't see well at all. Instead, they find food by making high-pitched cries and listening for the echoes. So, it's no surprise that some bats have huge ears!

MOUSE
Follow your nose

Mice are small mammals that search for scraps of food in nooks and crannies. They can smell much better than they see.

COW & HORSE

Eyes to the sides

These two plant-eaters have among the biggest fields of vision of all mammals. This helped their wild ancestors look out for predators approaching from the sides.

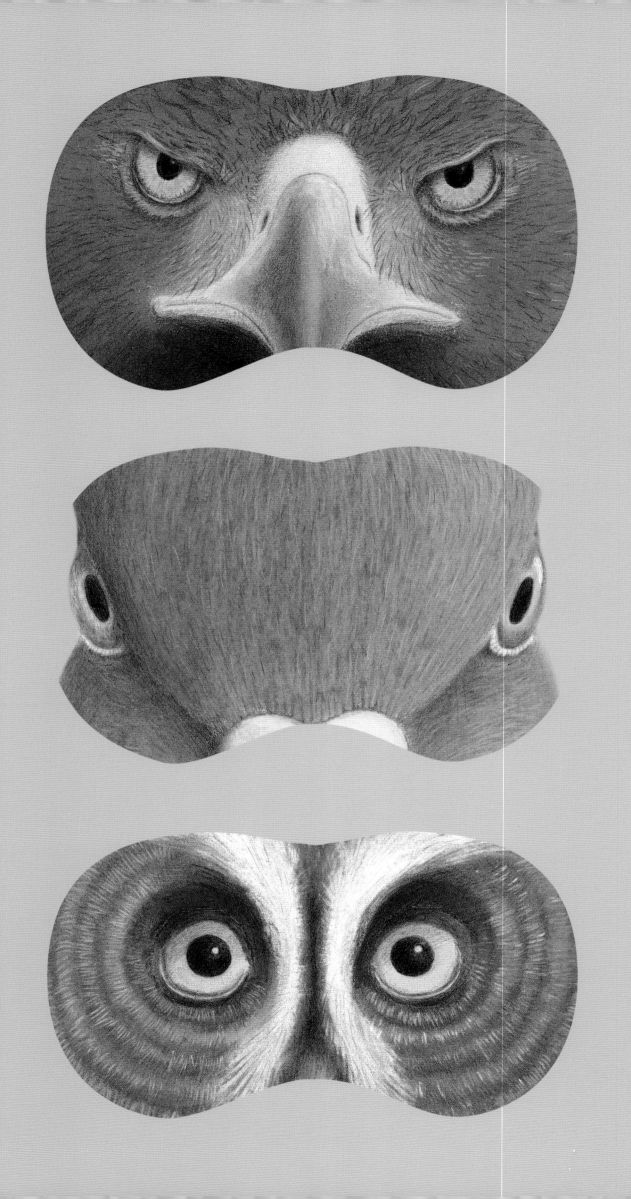

BIRDS
A WORLD OF MANY COLORS

Birds are vertebrates with bodies covered in feathers, a beak, and wings for flight. They also lay eggs. We know of about 9,000 bird species alive in the world today.

Protected behind three eyelids, birds' eyes are the most developed of all the vertebrates'. So, it's no surprise that vision is the most important sense for birds. They use their vision to move around, look out for predators, and snatch prey.

Hidden at the back of birds' retinas are incredible photoreceptors. Nocturnal birds have lots of rod cells for seeing in low-light conditions. Birds that are awake in the daytime have lots of cone cells to see vibrant colors. Most birds' cones contain tiny drops of yellow, red, or orange oil that filter light and increase the contrast between colors.

Many birds see more colors than mammals. This includes seeing ultraviolet light. That means that no matter what special ink is used to draw the scene, we humans can only imagine what birds see.

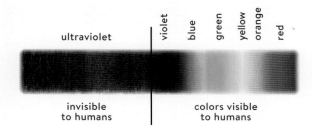

ultraviolet | violet | blue | green | yellow | orange | red

invisible to humans | colors visible to humans

EAGLE

There's a reason they call it eagle-eyed

Eagles are some of the greatest predators in the animal kingdom. Soaring high above mountain peaks, they can spot a mouse over half a mile away.

OWL

Eyes and ears

Owls are outstanding birds of prey in the day and, above all, at night. But as they silently fly over us, their two huge eyes are just part of the story.

PIGEON & HUMMINGBIRD
Amazing colors

You might not think that pigeons and hummingbirds have much in common, but they do. The vision of each of these birds is perfectly suited for the way they eat, find their way around, and spot predators.

WOODCOCK

Eyes in the back of its head?

Woodcocks have the largest field of vision of all the birds: 360 degrees, all the way around. They may not have eyes in the back of their head, but they really can see right behind them!

REPTILES, AMPHIBIANS, WORMS, AND MOLLUSKS
UNUSUAL WAYS TO SEE THE WORLD

This chapter brings together animals from lots of different groups:

Reptiles—vertebrates that lay eggs on land and have dry, scaly skin.
This group includes lizards, crocodiles, and snakes. We know of about 11,000 species of reptile.

Amphibians—vertebrates that live in water when they're young.
Most amphibians move onto land when they become adults. They lay clusters of eggs in lakes and rivers. We know of about 7,000 species of amphibian. Most of these are frogs.

Worms—long, thin animals without backbones.
They come in lots of forms, but annelids are the most familiar. Annelids are worms with bodies made of lots of identical segments. Earthworms are a common type of annelid found in every yard. We know of about 17,000 species of annelid.

Mollusks—a very varied group of animals with soft bodies.
Some produce hard shells while others don't. This group includes snails and slugs, as well as octopuses, clams, and many others. We know of about 85,000 species of mollusks.

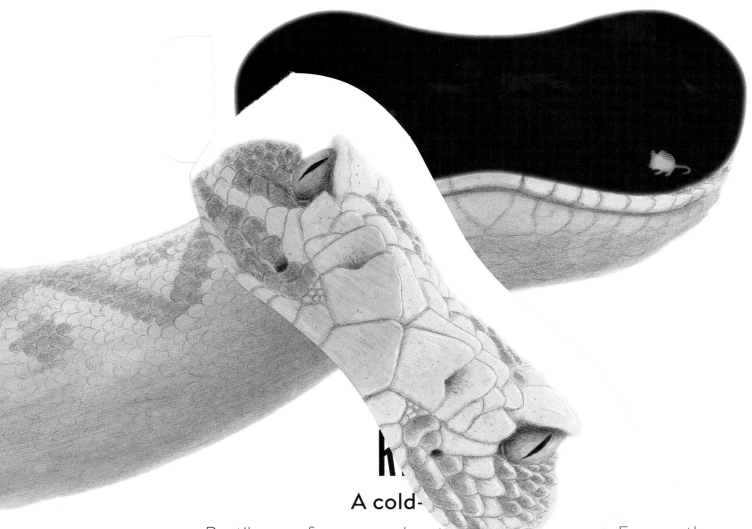

h...

A cold-

Reptiles see far more colors th... ...us. Eyes on the sides and near the top of their hea... ...them a wide visual field. At night, some reptiles complement their regular sight with heat vision for catching prey.

CHAMELEON
Two independent eyes

Vision is a chameleon's most powerful sense. Each of their eyes can turn separately in any direction. This allows them to look two different ways at the same time.

FROG

Blurred vision

Frogs' eyesight is not very strong. They use their vision very differently from the way we use ours. Even so, their simple way of seeing has made them successful animals.

EARTHWORM
Light and dark

These burrowing worms have long bodies made up of about a hundred segments. Each earthworm has a head, a mouth, and . . . five hearts! You might expect they'd have eyes as well, but earthworms are nearly blind.

SNAIL

A world in slow motion

Snails are mollusks with hard shells. Every snail has two tentacles on its head, with an eye at the end of each tentacle. These transmit visual information to the brain through a simple nervous system. The result: these mollusks can see, but badly.

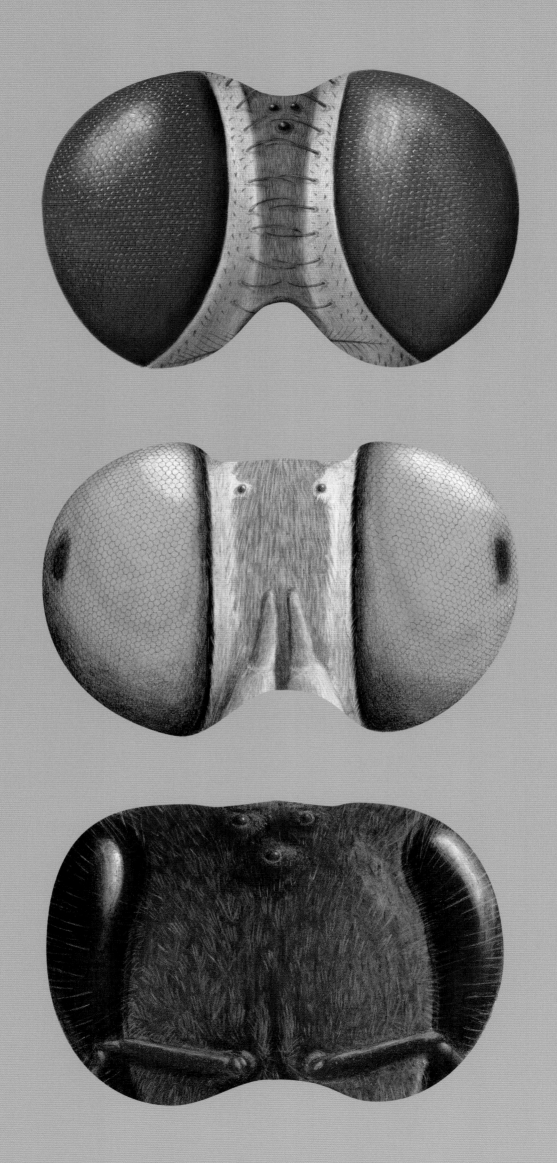

INSECTS
THOUSANDS OF EYES

Insects are the largest group in the animal kingdom. There are around a million known species. Among those are many kinds of bees, flies, dragonflies, butterflies, ants, mosquitoes, grasshoppers, and lots more. Insects have no backbones but a shell-like skeleton on the outside instead. This is called an exoskeleton. Every insect has six legs and three body parts. Most have wings too. Lots of insects first hatch from their eggs as wriggling wormlike larvae. But, over time, they can change their appearance completely.

Insects' senses work very differently from our own. For touch and taste, they have spindly antennae attached to their heads. The structure of their eyes is also very different. But strong vision is still important for insects. It helps to guide them in flight, find food, and identify members of their own species. Insects see much less clearly than we do. But, like many birds, they can often see ultraviolet rays. Plus, lots of them can spot tiny movements we would miss.

We're about to enter a whole new visual world.

The compound eye

Insects' eyes are called "compound" because they are made up of hundreds or thousands of miniature eyes. Each tiny eye, called an ommatidium, only sees the area right in front of it. But together, these tiny pictures form a bigger image of the world. More ommatidia in the eye means a more precise final image is put together. Ants have fewer than a hundred ommatidia, while a dragonfly's eye has 30,000.

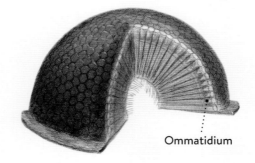

Ommatidium

Other members of the insects' larger group, the arthropods, also have compound eyes. Some examples are spiders, crabs, and millipedes.

BEE

Mosaic vision

Scientists have been studying bees for over a century, and they still have many questions about how they see. But they do know that bees have three simple eyes, as well as their two compound eyes. They call these tiny extra eyes ocelli. It must be remarkable to see the world with five eyes!

ANOTHER WAY TO SEE FLOWERS

Most birds and insects are able to see ultraviolet light. These are colors invisible to us. But for animals that can see them they reveal a rich visual world.

Many flowers develop ultraviolet patterns on their petals. These patterns are invisible to us but stand out to some animals, such as insects. The designs help insects to locate the flowers and even find a landing spot.

Lots of flowers rely on insects to help them reproduce, so there is a point to this. The insects carry bundles of the plant's cells, called pollen, from flower to flower. Wherever they drop it off, the pollen might help a seed develop. And this seed could then become a new plant. So, if the flower can attract more insects with an ultraviolet signpost, it has a better chance of reproducing. Isn't that incredible?

Below are pairs of images of the same flowers as seen by humans and bees. The left image shows what a human sees. The right image shows something like what the same flower might look like to a bee with ultraviolet vision.

Daisy
as seen by a human   as seen by an insect or bird

Daylily
human   insect or bird

Pincushion flower
human   insect or bird

Morning glory
human   insect or bird

Cinquefoil
human   insect or bird

Black-eyed Susan
human   insect or bird

FLY

Thousands of images at once

Flies can detect the smell of food many miles away. Their eyes can't see that far, but they do have great vision. Each compound eye is made up of 3,000 ommatidia. The fly's brain puts together the images from each ommatidium to make a single picture, like a jigsaw.

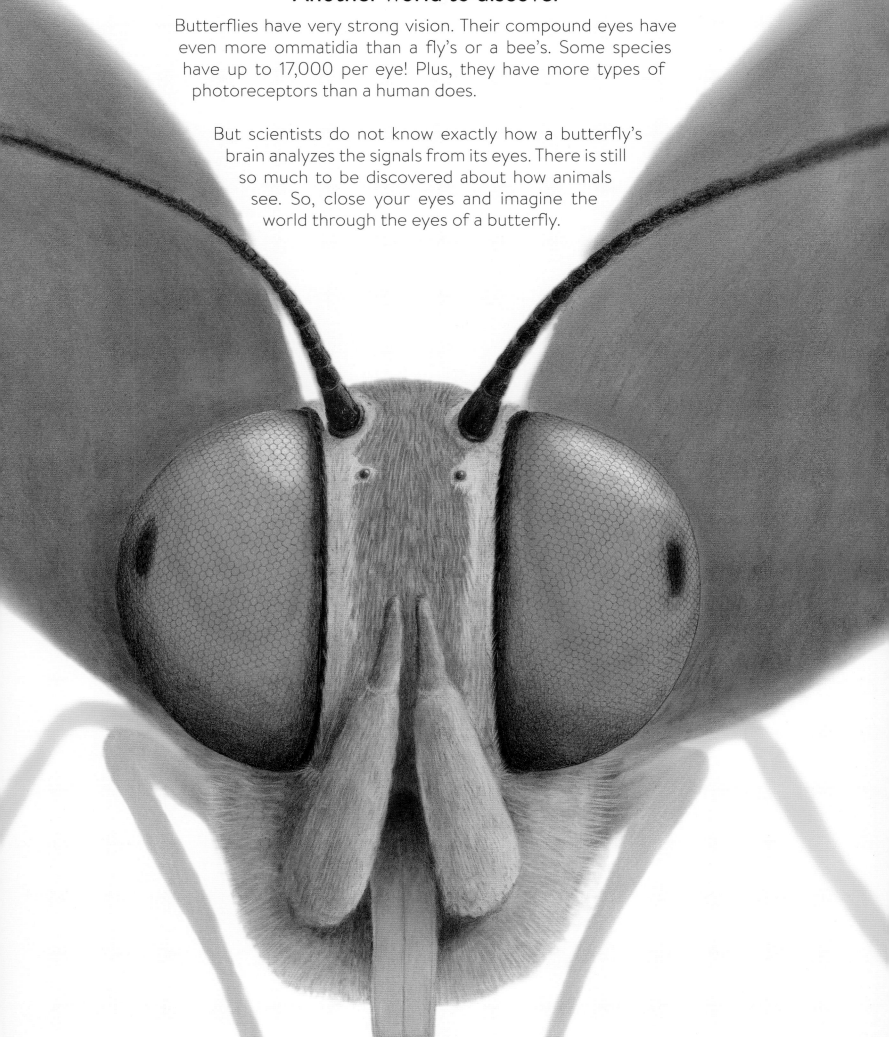

BUTTERFLY

Another world to discover

Butterflies have very strong vision. Their compound eyes have even more ommatidia than a fly's or a bee's. Some species have up to 17,000 per eye! Plus, they have more types of photoreceptors than a human does.

But scientists do not know exactly how a butterfly's brain analyzes the signals from its eyes. There is still so much to be discovered about how animals see. So, close your eyes and imagine the world through the eyes of a butterfly.

GLOSSARY

Compound eye
A special type of eye found among insects and their relatives. It is made up of hundreds or thousands of tiny eyes, called **ommatidia**. Together, these form a single picture.

Cone cells
Cells in the eye which detect different colors of light. They are one type of **photoreceptor**.

Dichromat
Animals which only see a mix of two colors. This is because they only have two types of **cone cells**.

Infrared
A color of light not visible to humans. Some reptiles see the infrared light given off by their prey, which helps them to hunt.

Ommatidia
The tiny individual eyes which make up a **compound eye**. There can be thousands of ommatidia in a compound eye.

Photoreceptors
Cells in the eye which are sensitive to light. They come in two types, **rod cells** and **cone cells**. An animal's brain analyzes signals from the photoreceptors to build a picture of the world.

Retina
The surface at the back of the eyeball. This is where the **photoreceptors** are located.

Rod cells
Cells in the eye which detect the intensity of light. They are one type of **photoreceptor**.

Trichromat
Animals which see a mix of three colors. They have three types of **cone cells**. Humans are trichromats.

Ultraviolet
A color of light not visible to humans. Many birds and insects can see ultraviolet light.

INDEX

List of sources

A note from the author:

Researching vision in general, and the vision of animals in particular, has been absolutely fascinating! The research for this book was spread over four years and several areas: ethology, biology, psychophysiology, veterinary studies, optics, physics, and perspective. All the information on animal vision comes primarily from scientific studies, as well as books with a more general approach.

Principal sources:

Bischof, Hans-Joachim. 2012. "Development of the visual system in birds and mammals," in *How Animals See the World: Comparative Behavior, Biology, and Evolution of Vision*: 483–500 (ed. Lazareva, Shimizu and Wasserman, Oxford University Press)

Bowmaker, James K. 2012. "Evolution of the vertebrate eye," in *How Animals See the World: Comparative Behavior, Biology, and Evolution of Vision*: 441–472 (ed. Lazareva, Shimizu and Wasserman, Oxford University Press)

Briscoe, Adriana D. and Chittka, Lars. 2001. "The evolution of color vision in insects," in *Annual Review of Entomology* 46: 471–510

Eckert, Roger. 2006. *Psychologie animale, mécanismes et adaptations* (de Boeck)

Gegenfurtner, Karl R. and Sharpe, Lindsay T (eds.). 2001. *Color Vision, from Genes to Perception* (Cambridge University Press)

Goldsmith, Timothy. 2007. "Ce que voient les oiseaux," in *Pour la science*: 354

Gregory, R. L. 1998. *Eye and Brain: The Psychology of Seeing* (Oxford University Press)

Hergueta, Stéphane. 2012. "Vision et évolution animale," Encyclopédie Universalis

Land, M. F. and Nilsson, D.-E. 2009. *Animal Eyes* (Oxford University Press)

Lazareva, Olga F., Shimizu, Toru, and Wasserman, Edward A. 2012. *How Animals See the World: Comparative Behavior, Biology, and Evolution of Vision* (Oxford University Press)

McFarland, David. 2001. *Le comportement animal: Psychobiologie, éthologie et évolution*, trans. d'Huart, Jacqueline (de Boeck)

Palmer, Stephen E. 1999. *Vision Science: Photons to Phenomenology* (MIT Press, Cambridge, Massachusetts, USA)

Pouliquen, Yves. 2011. *La transparence de l'œil* (Odile Jacob, Paris)

Rozenzweig, Mark R. and Leiman, Arnold. 1991. "La vision," in *Psychophysiologie*: 316–345 (Décarie, Québec)

Tanzarela, Stéphane. 2005. *Perception et communication chez les animaux* (de Boeck)

Tétry, Andrée. 1974. *Zoologie vol. III: métazoaires*: 653–666 (Gallimard la Pléiade, Paris)

Von Uexküll, Jacob. 2004. *Mondes animaux et monde humain* (Denoël, Paris)

Valeur, Bernard. 2011. *La couleur dans tous ses éclats*: 8–13 (Belin, Paris)

Author's acknowledgments

I'd like to thank Naomie for her valuable support in my utopias, as well as my family. An affectionate wink to Grand-père and his editorial advice. Thank you to the team at Seuil: Laurence Carrion, who had the great idea for the masks and who oversaw this project; Anne-Cécile Ferron for the amazing mock-up; Laure Bueno, Florence Pariente, and Claire Hartmann. I'd also like to thank the team at IGS.

What on Earth Books, The Black Barn, Wickhurst Farm,
Tonbridge, Kent TN11 8PS, United Kingdom

First published in France under the title: *Zooptique*
Copyright © 2012 Editions du Seuil, Paris, France

This edition first published in English by What on Earth Books in 2018
Translation copyright © 2018 What on Earth Publishing Ltd.

Written and illustrated by Guillaume Duprat
cosmologik.wordpress.com

Translated and edited by Patrick Skipworth

Consultant: Dr. Tadd Patton, Augusta University, Augusta, Georgia, USA

Library of Congress Cataloging-in-Publication Data available upon request

ISBN: 978-1-9998028-5-1

1 3 5 7 9 10 8 6 4 2

whatonearthbooks.com